The Spirit Within
&
the Intrinsic Stimuli

OGOCHUKWU V. NNAKWE

The Spirit Within & the Intrinsic Stimuli

Copyright © 2021 by Ogochukwu V. Nnakwe. All rights reserved. No portion of this book may be reproduced, stored in a retrieval system, or transmitted in any form or by any means, except for brief quotations in printed reviews, without prior permission of Ogochukwu V. Nnakwe. Requests may be submitted by email: vera.nnakwe@gmail.com.

Unless otherwise indicated, all Scripture verses are taken from the New King James Version®. Copyright © 1982 by Thomas Nelson. Used by permission. All rights reserved.

ISBN 978-1-7374303-1-5

Scripture quotations marked "NIV" are taken from THE HOLY BIBLE, NEW INTERNATIONAL VERSION®, NIV® Copyright © 1973, 1978, 1984, 2011 by Biblica, Inc.® Used by permission. All rights reserved worldwide.

Scripture quotations marked "MEV" are taken from the Modern English Version. Copyright © 2014 by Military Bible Association. Used by permission. All rights reserved.

Scripture quotations marked "JUB" are taken from the Jubilee Bible, copyright © 2000, 2001, 2010, 2013 by Life Sentence Publishing, Inc. Used by permission of Life Sentence Publishing, Inc., Abbotsford, Wisconsin. All rights reserved.

Scripture quotations marked "ESV" are taken from The ESV® Bible (The Holy Bible, English Standard Version®). ESV® Text Edition: 2016. Copyright © 2001 by Crossway, a publishing ministry of Good News Publishers. The ESV® text has been reproduced in cooperation with and by permission of Good News Publishers. Unauthorized reproduction of this publication is prohibited. All rights reserved.

Scripture quotations marked "CEV" are taken from the Contemporary English Version®

Copyright © 1995 American Bible Society. All rights reserved.

Editing, formatting, and cover design by ChristianEditingandDesign.com.

Table of Contents

God, Your Way Maker	7
Live on Purpose, Live Fearlessly	9
You Bear the Image of Your Creator	13
The Promised Land	17
Before God, Nothing is Impossible	19
Trusting God and Waiting on Him	21
He Has a Plan	23
Prophesy Over Your Life	25
He Knows Your Name	27
You Are Free	29
Your Restorations	31
Be Still and Know that He is God	33
Overcoming the Goliath	35
Peace in the Midst of the Storm	37
Don't Give Up	39
Pray Like Jabez	41
Set Your Goal and Fix Your Eye on Your Goals	43
Count Your Blessings	45
References	47

Preface

The spirit within has a powerful internal force, an intrinsic stimulus that drives it to doing something for an inherent satisfaction. When the spirit within is stimulated and motivated intrinsically, it develops the willpower, the backbone, that ignites a desire to be your best self and not dependent on extrinsic stimuli motivated by external reward. As a child of God, it is important that the spirit within is motivated by an intrinsic stimulus and not by an extrinsic one. When the spirit within is moved by intrinsic stimuli, you don't give up on yourself or your dream when support is not forthcoming from your family and friends; you don't give up when faced with challenges or lose hope when faced with rejection or criticism. When the spirit within is motivated intrinsically, you encourage yourself when you don't feel encouraged. You surround yourself with people who are supportive of your ideas and dreams and move away from toxic and unfriendly environments. You set goals and seek opportunities, determined to see positive rewards. You don't grow weary when you don't see immediate results because you trust and believe that God's time is the best, and in due time God will manifest Himself.

No matter what you go through or where you see yourself in life, if the spirit within does not "internally" motivate you to believe in yourself, to believe in your God, to dream big, to take actions to achieve your dreams, to step up and step out in faith, you will continue to doubt yourself and the ability of God, your Creator. If you trust God and believe in the abilities He placed in your life, you don't worry when you don't have approval from people. God created you for a purpose, and He desires to see you live life to your full potential. He affirmed this in Jeremiah 29:11: "For I know the plans I have for you. . . . plans to prosper you and not to harm you, plans to give you hope and a future" (NIV). Let your spirit within believe His Word, "for we walk by faith, not by sight" (2 Corinthians 5:7). By doing so, you have built your faith and hope on the solid Rock, Jesus Christ, so that no matter what is happening around you, you will stay strong.

God, Your Way Maker

Isaiah 51:15 says, "I am the LORD your God who divided the sea whose waves roared" (MEV). Yes, He is the great "I AM." He is the unchangeable God! He is the unshakable God! He is the Alpha and the Omega! Just as He commanded Moses and parted the Red Sea so that the Israelites could cross, He will part your ways for you. He will clear every stumbling block keeping you from crossing over to your promised land, every stumbling block keeping you from reaching your destiny or fulfilling your calling and God's purpose in your life. Every hand attempting to stop God's promise in your life will have the experience of the Egyptian army in the middle of the Red Sea, when Moses lifted his arms again and the sea closed up on them (see Exodus 14).

God made a way for Joseph in the book of Genesis. God lifted him up from pit to palace. When his brothers wanted to get rid of him, they did not know they were setting him up to successfully reach his destiny. Although his journey to the palace was not easy, the end result was glorious (see Genesis 40–45). He kept his faith in God strong and God saw him through. So do not be weary in your spirit regardless of the challenges you face. Let your spirit within keep you strong in your faith. God will surely see you through.

As God made a way for Daniel out of the lions' den (see Daniel 6) and for Esther to save her people (see Esther 5), He will make ways for you. There are many other places in the Bible where God showed His greatness in the lives of His people. He made ways for them, and these should be proof to us that He is the Way Maker.

In Isaiah 40:4, God says he will make the "crooked places . . . straight." Our God makes a way in the wilderness and a "path through the mighty waters." He has promised He will do new things that will spring forth, and you will see it (see Isaiah 43:16–19).

Live on Purpose, Live Fearlessly

Many times, you desire to do something new. You have big dreams and ambitions of what you want to be in life, but fear holds you back from taking a step of faith forward—fear of uncertainty, of failure, of what people will say, especially family and friends who know your background. Those people fail to see the new you; they are not looking at the same level you are. Your vision is yours and not theirs. People can say whatever they think about other people. It's part of nature. People are entitled to their own thinking and feelings about one another. How someone treats you and makes you feel is their own personal business. The most important thing is how you take those thoughts and feelings. Do you take in those negativities, or do you brush them off to set your eyes on your goals? Do you dwell on the negativity from people and allow it to put fear in you? Do you allow it to disturb your peace and keep you from moving forward? Let your spirit within be strong! Be spirited! When you are determined to live on purpose, your spirit should be strong to live fearlessly. You should not let fear of what people will say keep you from making a change to invest in yourself and improve your life. Brush off any negative treatment from people. Channel your thoughts and focus your energy on the positive things. Don't let your spirit be drained of ways to be creative to improve your life.

If you want to live on purpose and live fearlessly, you have to be in charge of your life; you have to be in the driver's seat, trusting God to lead the way. Your spirit within has to intrinsically keep on keeping on and pushing forward. If you allow people to be in the driver's seat of your life, they will drive you in the direction they feel is suitable for them, where they use you to fulfill their desires and personal goals. Then they leave you desolate. A spirit-filled child of God, motivated intrinsically, depends on God to lead his or her way and is cautiously vigilant in dealing with people so as not to be misled.

When you live fearlessly and your spirit within is motivated to live on purpose, you decide what is best for you. Sometimes you may have a great idea of starting a business or inventing something, but you feel like consulting someone you think is knowledgeable and wise enough to give you some suggestions. That is okay, but the final decision rests with you. The spirit within you has to believe that you can do this, that you can start the business and be successful. You can pursue your dreams and, with God on your side, you will live to your highest potential. You have to remind yourself that you are in charge of your life, and you have to run your own race. The apostle Paul says in 1 Corinthians 9:24, "Do you not know that those who run in a race all run, but one receives the prize? Run in such a way that you may obtain it." So, you have to be in the driver's seat of your life, to be in charge of how you want to live, trusting God to lead the way.

You don't have to be the strongest person or wait until you have it all before you decide to live on purpose and fearlessly. You have to be bold and take a step of faith to pursue that dream, even when you don't know what the outcome will be.

Chadwick Boseman put it this way: "Fearlessness means taking the first step, even if you don't know where it will take you. It means being driven by a higher purpose. It means knowing that you reveal your character when you stand apart, more than when you stand with the crowd."[1]

When you choose to live on purpose, your spirit within decides not to let fear of rejection keep you from moving on. Do not let it keep you from striving to find God's purpose for your life. As Chadwick Boseman said above, "You reveal your character when you stand apart, more than when you stand with the crowd." If you belong to any group that does not bring out the best of God's purpose for your life, you have to leave it. Leaving the group does not mean you don't like or love them; you are leaving because continuing to stay constrains you from fulfilling God's calling in your life. You don't have to reduce your worth or suppress the spirit of God in you by trying to be accepted. Move on. God will bring you people who accept you for who you are, for being yourself.

*Will Smith puts it this way: "Don't chase people. Be yourself, do your own thing and work hard. The right people, the ones who really belong in your life will come to you and stay."*²

When you are living on purpose and fearlessly, you don't let anyone control your mind, thoughts, feelings, or emotions. "For the Spirit God gave us does not make us timid, but gives us power, love, and self-discipline" (2 Timothy 1:7 NIV).

You Bear the Image of Your Creator

Everything created by God is good, including you (see 1 Timothy 4:4). You are created by God in His own image, in His likeness. You're bearing the image of God, your Creator. Don't let any spirit that is not of God tell you otherwise. You're perfect the way God created you. Don't let anyone tell you or make you feel like you are not good enough. You are a child of the most high God. You look just like your Father in heaven. You carry the image of your Creator. Let your spirit within rejoice and be glad for who you are. You are the chosen generation, anointed and equipped. Your spirit within has to believe this, accept it, and be motivated by it. Even if you have never received a compliment in your life, compliment yourself. Remind yourself daily of whose you are and esteem yourself as such. God wants you to know today that you are enough in Him:

You're good enough.

You're perfect enough.

You're beautiful enough.

You're handsome enough.

You're wise enough.

You're tall enough.

You're healthy enough.

You're strong enough.

You're intelligent enough.

You're smart enough.

You're worthy enough.

You're knowledgeable enough.

You're qualified enough.

You're just enough as God Almighty, your Creator, wants you to be. Embrace yourself and the work of God in your life. Let your spirit within be intrinsically motivated daily to strive to be the best you can in all you do. Don't wait or dwell on extrinsic reward, compliment, or motivation, so that even if you did not get them from anyone, you would be content within yourself for who you are and whose you are. God created you for a purpose. Try to find God's purpose for your life and live based on His purpose for you. Don't let the spirit of doubt, fear, maltreatment, intimidation, or rejection take your mind away from staying focused on your goals. Ignore the naysayers, bullies, tormenters, persecutors, and oppressors. Keep your eyes fixed on Jesus. Keep them fixed on your goals, dreams, and ambitions. No matter how big or small your dreams are, no matter the challenges, just believe that "with God all things are possible" (Matthew 19:26).

Be careful about the kinds of associations you keep. A group you belong to should be the type in which you have the opportunity to grow as a person, and you hear positive, encouraging words. The people within such a group are oppositive influencers, with a common goal to uplift and support each other to become their best selves.

Surround yourself with people who are happy to see you succeed in life, who value your worth, respect you, and treat you with love and kindness; people who do not diminish your worth, belittle you, or think of themselves as more important than you.

When your spirit within is intrinsically motivated, you will not worry about family and friends who try to isolate you and make you feel alone. You know that you're not alone, for "one with God is a majority," as Martin Luther said. Leave the battle in God's hands; God will fight your battle, and He will see you through.

The Promised Land

"The LORD your God is bringing you into a good land, a land of brooks of water, of fountains and springs, that flow out of valleys and hills" (Deuteronomy 8:7). This is the word of the Lord for you. As a child of God, you have the spirit of the Lord living within you, and you have to believe in the promises of God to see its manifestation.

"We walk by faith, not by sight" (2 Corinthians 5:7). When God promised the Israelites the promised land, they had to leave Egypt, where they lived in slavery. They went on a journey to get to the promised land. Sometimes, you might need to relocate to get to your promised land. You might need to make a move to bring change. You might need to rearrange things around you, from the usual to the unusual, to see a change you want.

When you are motivated by intrinsic stimuli and you believe in God's promise in Deuteronomy 8:7, you hold onto your faith, knowing that Jesus loves you and cares for you. Even in the midst of trials and tribulations, you will not lose hope. You will not give up on your dreams or lose sight of your life's ambitions. You trust your inner self not to be moved by the things on the outside because you know that the Lord God Almighty, whom you serve, makes His light shine upon you. When you trust God and do not doubt His abilities, He will be moved by your faith and will open doors of greatness, favor, opportunities, divine intervention, divine connections, healing, restoration, and breakthrough. What else could you ask for if these promises become your portion? You will relax and enjoy the unquenchable flow of peace, happiness, and joy God has bestowed on your life.

Before God, Nothing is Impossible

"He has made the earth by His power, He has established the world by His wisdom" (Jeremiah 10:12). There's nothing too difficult for God, the Creator of heaven and earth. As a child of God, this should be the confidence you have in God. No matter your present condition, whether good or bad, believe that the Creator of the universe knows how to turn your situation around for good. Believe that the forces that are for you are greater than the forces that are against you. Because your spirit within is not moved by or dependent on external stimuli, you believe that "with God nothing is impossible" (Luke 1:37 JUB).

Trusting God and Waiting on Him

"Those who wait on the LORD Shall renew their strength; They shall mount up with wings like eagles, They shall run and not be weary, They shall walk and not faint" (Isaiah 40:31). This is the word of the Lord for you. In all your endeavors, put your trust in God. Even when the going gets tough and you feel like giving up, don't give up. Keep on keeping on; keep pushing hard, as hard as your strength can take you. It's not over until God says it's over.

The Lord God Almighty is your strength. He is with you, working within you even when you don't see Him working. Just keep believing God and trusting Him in your endeavors. As a child of God, be motivated intrinsically to trust God with all your heart. You trust Him not because your pastor or priest is leading you in church faith but because you love God from the bottom of your heart and you want to serve Him all the days of your life. So, when your pastor or priest is not there, you will still be strong in your faith because you trust in God and not in people.

The Spirit Within & the Intrinsic Stimuli

The Word of the Lord reminds us in Proverbs 3:5–6, "Trust in the LORD with all your heart, And lean not on your own understanding; In all your ways acknowledge Him, and He shall direct your paths." Numbers 23:19 says, "God is not a man, that He should lie, Nor a son of man, that He should repent. Has He said, and will He not do?" If God said He will do something, He will do it, and as a child of God inspired by internal stimuli, the spirit within you, you have to believe these words in your life.

He Has a Plan

"For I know the thoughts that I think toward you, says the LORD, thoughts of peace and not of evil, to give you a future and a hope" (Jeremiah 29:11). This is the word of the Lord for you. God knows how to bring this promise to fulfillment. Stay positive and be determined to find God's purpose for your life. Commit to it and stay focused. Invest in whatever dreams God has put in your heart. In due time, God will perfect you. He will establish you, and for all your tears, sorrows, disappointments, humiliations, and pain, He will turn things around and shower you with everlasting joy to the glory of His mighty name.

As a child of God who trusts your inner self with strong faith in the words of the Lord, you should know that if God says that His plan for your life is of good and not of evil, you know that anything bad or unpleasant is not God's plan for you. Therefore, you should not settle for it or accept it as part of your life. You should pray against it and ask God to deal with the situation. This will help you stand firm on your faith.

The Spirit Within & the Intrinsic Stimuli

When your spirit within believes that God's Word, which says His plan for you is to prosper you and to give you hope and a future, you should not allow external voices or treatment from people make you feel otherwise. Focus on your internal instincts to help you push through every obstacle on your way until you accomplish the plans and the purpose of God in your life.

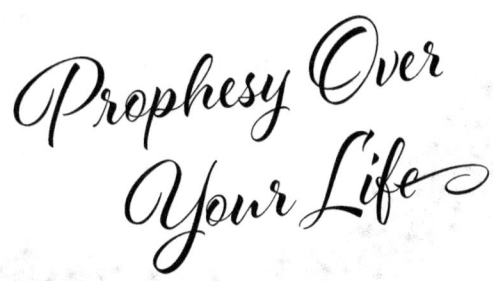

Prophesy Over Your Life

Ezekiel 37:1–14 tells us that the dry bones shall live again! Prophesy over your life! This is the word of the Lord for you. What is it in your life that seems to have dried up? Speak to that condition, to that dream that seems too big to attain. God wants you to speak life into that dead situation. Speak to it and believe that all hope is not gone. As long as there's life, there's hope.

Speak as the Spirit of the Lord leads you. As you begin to command, let breath enter, let there be rattling sounds of life coming into your life, finances, health, destiny, future, and family. Let the scattered bones in your life begin to come together bone-to-bone. Be positive and speak positive words over your life, and believe it. This activates the power of the sovereign Lord God Almighty to manifest Himself and to bring His promises to fulfillment.

Every child of God who strongly believes in the spirit within and is motivated intrinsically knows that there is power in the words. You pray daily, you prophesy over your life, and you trust God to answer you. Even when you ask a pastor or priest to pray for you, if you do not exercise the power of right believing, you might still go home the same. There is power in believing in your faith. In many places in the Bible where Jesus performed miracles, one interesting point is that Jesus always asks them, "Do you believe?" Then He goes on to heal the person.

Jesus says if we believe in our hearts without doubt, and we tell a mountain to move and "be cast into the sea," it will be done (see Mark 11:23). He also tells us that if we believe when we pray, it will be answered (see Mark 11:24). This is the authority given to you as a child of God; all you need is to exercise it.

He Knows Your Name

God is the Lord your God; He knows you by your name. He will open before you "the double doors, So that the gates will not be shut: 'I will go before you And make the crooked places straight; I will break in pieces the gates of bronze And cut the bars of iron. I will give you treasures And hidden riches of secret places" (Isaiah 45:1–3). This is the word of the Lord for you. God is reaffirming His promises to you. In Jeremiah 1:5, God says that "before I formed you in [your mother's] womb I knew you; Before you were born, I sanctified you; I ordained you a prophet to the nations." Let your spirit within continue to believe strongly in these positive affirmations. Even when you go through some tough situations in life and you wonder why, I want you to know that God has not forgotten you. He cares about you and all that concerns you.

Staying positive and keeping a positive mind-set is the key. It unlocks your inner strength. Be motivated intrinsically. Doing so will give you the ability to think critically and creatively. It will give you the ability to hold on strongly to your faith in God.

You Are Free

For whom Jesus, the Son of God, sets free is free indeed (see John 8:36)! Believe you are free! You need to remind yourself that you're free from anything holding your mind and thoughts captive in bad feelings and emotions based on what happened in the past and what is currently happening in your life. Sometimes certain things happen that bring different kinds of thoughts and memories. Those bad memories, negative feelings, and emotions can stifle your mind and keep you from thinking clearly. They can keep you from thinking positively and letting go of your past. When you let go of your past, you embrace the present and apply the power of resilience; this enables you to continue to push forward, trusting and believing God for a brighter future and a better you.

You have to believe that if Jesus, the Son of God, sets you free, you are free indeed. You are free from bondage, shackles, chains, curses, allegations, accusations, pain, self-pity, self-blame, and doubt. You're free! This is the word of the Lord for you. Believe you're free! Free your mind and yourself from anything holding you back from moving forward and striving to be your best. Let your spirit within believe in the inner strength you draw from God. You "are more than conquerors through Him who loved us" (Romans 8:37).

Your Restorations

"'All those who devour you shall be devoured; And all your adversaries, every one of them, shall go into captivity; Those who plunder you shall become plunder, And all who prey upon you I will make a prey. For I will restore health to you And heal you of your wounds,' says the LORD" (Jeremiah 30:16–17). This is the word of the Lord for you. God will restore your health and everything that may affect your health in one way or another. He will restore your peace.

Let your spirit within believe that God will turn all your tears and troubles into testimonies, your trials to triumphs, your disappointments to appointments. He will turn your sadness and sorrow into joy and praises. Believe and continue to stay strong in your faith in God.

Be Still and Know that He is God

Psalm 46:1–10 tells us variously: The Lord is with you; God is your refuge. Do not be afraid even when the mountains shake and crumble into the raging, roaring sea. God is a river who never runs dry. He helps us in times of turmoil and trouble. Those who dwell with Him will not be moved. Be still and know that He is God. This is the word of the Lord for you, especially in this time when so many nations are faced with unrest.

During this time, let your spirit be strong and your faith unwavering. Continue to stay strong in your faith in God; He will be your refuge, strength, provider, protector, and restorer.

Overcoming the Goliath

Stand your ground and declare with confidence in God against the Goliath in your life! Declare like David did when he was faced with Goliath. David said to Goliath, "You come to me with a sword, with a spear, and with a javelin. But I come to you in the name of the LORD of hosts, the God of the armies of Israel, whom you have defied" (1 Samuel 17:45).

Many things can become Goliaths in our lives. Sometimes it can be life situations that seem too big to overcome. Sometimes it can be someone standing in your way of living the fulfilling life you were created for. The Goliath can be anything that puts fear in you or anyone who suppresses you and your joy or intimidates you. It can be anyone who bullies or belittles you and always tries to overpower you.

When your spirit within is strong in your faith in God, you don't allow external pressure to put you down. Stand your ground in prayer and declare with confidence in God. Refuse to allow situations to keep you from pushing forward. Irrespective of how giant Goliath was, David did not let that put fear in him. Act like David!

Do not let how badly someone treated you put fear in you. Although you cannot change someone's attitude toward you, you can change how you react and respond to them. Keep a positive mind-set no matter the challenges. Believe in your inner spirit and be strong for yourself. You will triumph and overcome. Believing in yourself and your inner spirit and being motivated by intrinsic stimuli will help you maintain good mental health and emotional well-being. It will help you build your confidence in God.

Peace in the Midst of the Storm

Like Jesus, you can have peace in the midst of the storm (see Matthew 8:24–27). Keep your faith strong and try your best to maintain your peace in the midst of the storm, no matter how furious the storm is.

Sometimes in life you meet different kinds of challenges; some might take you by surprise and some might not. Anything that is beyond your control, you must commit to the hands of God Almighty. Staying steadfast in your prayers and maintaining a peaceful mind-set allows you to trust God completely, believing in Him to act on your storm. These are good attributes of a child of God whose spirit within is motivated by internal forces. They activate God's power and allow Him to move in your direction.

God wants you to have strong faith in Him, to believe He is capable of handling that situation. He is capable of rebuking the winds and the waves to calm that storm in your life. Trust that God will do it for you. He is still the I AM. He created the whole universe by the words of His mouth. The winds and the waves of life must obey Him because they do not come to pass if God has not spoken. He will surely see you through.

Don't Give Up

Don't give up! Sometimes in life, you might encounter certain situations and moments where you feel like giving up. Sometimes they might be emotional or physical encounters with unpleasant experiences. Despite the struggles of this life, disappointments, bad breaks, health problems, failures, financial problems, and so on, do not give up! Although giving up might seem to be the easy way out, it should not be your only option. Let your spirit within be motivated intrinsically so that you maintain unwavering faith.

Do not give up pursuing your dreams even when things are not turning out the way you hoped or expected. Do not give up when you feel overwhelmed because you have not accomplished your goals. It's okay to take a break, recalibrate, recharge, and refuel your energy, but do not give up.

Though challenges, trials, and tribulations may come, know that "the steadfast love of the Lord never ceases" (Lamentations 3:22 ESV). "God's love never fails" (Psalm 136:1 CEV). So, cheer up and remind yourself that God is always with you. He has given you the strength to overcome, triumph, and excel.

Though you may stumble, you will not fall, for the Lord God Almighty upholds you in His hand (see Psalm 37:24). Keep fighting for your life. Keep fighting for your salvation. Keep fighting for your dreams, and don't give up. Be confident in your God, knowing that He who began the work in you will carry it to completion (see Philippians 1:6). Failure is not the end of the world. Get up and keep moving. Be strong and courageous. Stand strong on your faith in God; He will be your guard (see 1 Corinthians 16:13). Be strong and do not give up, for God will reward your hard work (see 2 Chronicles 15:7).

Pray Like Jabez

The God who answered Jabez, let Him be my God! "Jabez called on the God of Israel saying, 'Oh, that You would bless me indeed, and enlarge my territory, that Your hand would be with me, and that You would keep me from evil, that I may not cause pain!' So God granted him what he requested" (1 Chronicles 4:10).

Pray like Jabez and believe that God will change your life for good. He will expand your boarders. He is still the I AM. He has not changed. He is more than able to take away your pain, shame, and sorrow.

What is the label you carry? What are the labels people, family, or friends placed on you? What does your name signify? Jabez's mother gave birth to him in pain, and that was the significance of his name (see 1 Chronicles 4:9). The spirit within Jabez was motivated intrinsically to believe that his name should not determine his destiny. Jabez believed in whose he is. He believed that God had the final say in his life, so he sought the face of the Lord, and God changed his destiny for good.

The Spirit Within & the Intrinsic Stimuli

You may have been given different names that put you in a box, and the forces that follow those names keep you from moving forward in life. Refuse to accept any negative meaning behind your name. Refuse to allow a label people placed on you to control you. You may have been deemed incompetent, a failure, or unqualified. Let your spirit within be motivated intrinsically so that you don't dwell on the negative things of your life. Rather, run after God, who created you in His own image. Try your best to be your best, and God will surely see you through.

Set Your Goal and Fix Your Eye on Your Goals

As a child of God, you should always have short-term and long-term goals of what you want in your life and what you want to achieve. It is always good to set goals at the beginning of the year and then, after six months, assess whether you are on track. Also make a yearly assessment to determine if you met the goals and what might need to be adjusted. When you are motivated internally to do what is best for you and you have the hunger to become your very best in life, the goals you set will become your passion. Every year, ensure you have a new resolution. What are your New Year's resolutions? Have you set your goals for the year? If not, it isn't too late to start.

If you did not accomplish some of your goals from the previous year, don't lose hope. Reassess to figure out what approach worked well and what did not work; then try to do something differently this time around.

Setting goals starts with planning, then taking actions toward the goals. Remember: a dream without an action plan is just a dream. I encourage you to dream big and take a step of faith, an action toward achieving that dream. Look for every possible opportunity, trusting God to make ways for you where there seems to be none. You just have to keep moving forward, trying your best in all your endeavors.

I declare that the Lord God will be your helper and the sustainer of your soul (see Psalm 54:4). In this year, the Lord God Almighty will deliver you from the sword of pharaoh (see Exodus 18:4). Who will condemn you when the Lord is your helper (see Isaiah 50:9)? No one! I declare His words in Psalm 18:35: May God cover you with the shield of His salvation, may He uphold you with His right hand, and may His gentleness make you great, in Jesus's name, Amen.

Count Your Blessings

A spirit-filled child of God is the one who acknowledges God and lives a life of gratitude. Your spirit within is internally motivated to always be grateful to God for His grace and mercies over your life, regardless of your present condition. You don't wait to be extrinsically motivated before you can show gratitude. Count your blessings and name them one by one. No matter how challenging things may have been for you, please, find something in your life that God has done for you and be grateful for it. At least you're alive and breathing in the land of the living! Remember: it is only the living who can praise God (see Isaiah 38:19). There's hope for tomorrow. Cheer up and continue to PUSH (pray until something happens).

References

1. Boseman, Chadwick, quoted in Jarren Smith. "Chadwick Boseman Redefined 'Doing It for the Culture.'" Posted September 1, 2020. *The Famuan*. http://www.thefamuanonline.com/2020/09/01/chadwick-boseman-redefined-doing-it-for-the-culture/.

2. Smith, Will. "Will Smith Quotes." *QuoteFancy*. https://quotefancy.com/quote/933767/Will-Smith-Don-t-chase-people-Be-yourself-do-your-own-thing-and-work-hard-The-right.

www.ingramcontent.com/pod-product-compliance
Lightning Source LLC
Chambersburg PA
CBHW061303040426
42444CB00010B/2496